Pizza Cookbook for Beginner's

Essential Guide to Homemade Pizza Making

BY

Carla Hale

Copyright 2019 Carla Hale

License Notes

No part of this Book can be reproduced in any form or by any means including print, electronic, scanning or photocopying unless prior permission is granted by the author.

All ideas, suggestions and guidelines mentioned here are written for informative purposes. While the author has taken every possible step to ensure accuracy, all readers are advised to follow information at their own risk. The author cannot be held responsible for personal and/or commercial damages in case of misinterpreting and misunderstanding any part of this Book

Table of Contents

Introduction 5

   Skillet Primavera Pizza 7

   Mediterranean Pesto Pizza 10

   Skillet BBQ Chicken Pizza 12

   Mexican Pizza 15

   Veggie Vegetarian Pizza 18

   Vegetable Pizza 21

   Low Carb Breakfast Pizza 24

   Thai Chicken Pizza 27

   Pickle Pizza 29

   Spinach and Alfredo Pizza 32

   Four Cheese Margherita Pizza 35

   Sausage Pizza Sliders 37

   Classic Chicken Alfredo Pizza 39

   Pizza Nachos 43

Deep Dish Alfredo Pizza 45

Loaded Pizza Stromboli 48

Classic New York Pizza 51

Chicken Pizza Burgers 54

Beer Pizza 57

Barbecue Chicken Pizza Sliders 60

Ham, Egg and Cheese Pizza 63

Breakfast Cornbread Pizza 65

Miniature Deep Dish Pizzas 68

Pizza Puffs 70

Mac and Cheese Pizza 73

Conclusion 76

Author's Afterthoughts 77

About the Author 78

Introduction

There is no other highly popular dish served in the United States then pizza. What is there not to like about pizza? A savory dough topped off with tomato sauce and a bucket-load of cheese, pizza is the ultimate dish for any picky eater in your home. For children, pizza is often counted as one of their favorite foods while for adults, it is counted as one of the most convenient meals around. From the ability to add your favorite toppings, there is rarely a type of pizza that isn't loved by at least one person.

If you love pizza and have always wanted to make pizza within the comfort of your own home, then you have certainly come to the right place. Inside of this in depth pizza cookbook, you will learn every aspect of pizza making, from making the dough correctly, to rising the dough, preparing the sauce to even pairing the pizza with the perfect toppings. By the end of this book and with the help of over 25 pizza recipes, I hope that you will become a pizza making pro in no time.

So, let's stop wasting time and get to cooking!

Skillet Primavera Pizza

This is an incredibly easy pizza dish you can make whenever you are craving pizza. Feel free to top off with your favorite toppings for the tastiest results.

Makes: 6 servings

Total Prep Time: 45 minutes

Ingredients:

- 2 red bell peppers, thinly sliced
- ½ of a head of broccoli, chopped into florets
- ¼ of a red onion, thinly sliced
- 1 cup of cherry tomatoes, cut into halves
- Dash of salt and black pepper
- 1 to 2 Tbsp. of extra virgin olive oil
- All-purpose flour, for dusting
- 1 pound of pizza dough
- 1 cup of ricotta cheese
- 1 cup of mozzarella cheese, shredded

Directions:

1. Preheat the oven to 400 degrees.

2. On a baking sheet, add the sliced red bell peppers, broccoli florets, sliced red onion and cherry tomato halves. Toss well to mix. Season with a dash of salt and black pepper.

3. Place into the oven to roast for 20 minutes or until soft. Remove and set aside.

4. Increase the temperature of the oven to 500 degrees.

5. Dust a flat surface with flour. Place the pizza dough onto the surface. Roll until 8 inches in diameter. Transfer into a cast iron skillet. Grease the top of the dough with the olive oil.

6. Add dollops of the ricotta cheese onto the dough. Sprinkle half of the mozzarella cheese over the top.

7. Top off with the roasted vegetables. Drizzle 1 tablespoon of the olive oil over the veggies. Season with a dash of salt and black pepper.

8. Place into the oven to bake for 10 to 12 minutes or until the crust is golden.

9. Remove and serve immediately.

Mediterranean Pesto Pizza

If you love the taste of Mediterranean cuisine, then this is a pizza dish I know you will fall in love with. Serve with pita flatbreads for the tastiest results.

Makes: 2 servings

Total Prep Time: 15 minutes

Ingredients:

- 2 Tbsp. of pesto, prepared
- 2, 6 inch Greek pita flatbreads
- ½ cup of feta cheese, crumbled
- 2 tomatoes, chopped
- 8 Kalamata olives, pits removed

Directions:

1. Heat up the oven to 350 degrees.

2. Spread the prepared pesto on top of each pita flatbreads.

3. Top off with the crumbled feta cheese, chopped tomatoes and Kalamata olives.

4. Transfer the flatbreads onto the baking sheet.

5. Place into the oven to bake for 8 to 10 minutes.

6. Remove and serve immediately.

Skillet BBQ Chicken Pizza

This is the perfect pizza dish to make during your next football watching event. Slightly spicy in taste, this is a pizza dish I know you will love.

Makes: 2 servings

Total Prep Time: 45 minutes

Ingredients:

- 1 Tbsp. of extra virgin olive oil, extra for brushing
- ½ pound of chicken breasts, boneless, skinless and cut into small cubes
- Dash of salt and black pepper
- 1 pound of pizza dough
- 2 Tbsp. of barbecue sauce, extra for drizzling
- ½ cup of cheddar cheese, shredded
- ½ cup of fontina, shredded
- ¼ of a red onion, sliced thinly
- Ranch dressing, for drizzling
- Chives, chopped and for garnish

Directions:

1. Preheat the oven to 525 degrees.

2. In a skillet set over medium to high heat, add in the olive oil. Add in the chicken breast cubes. Cook for 8 to 10 minutes or until golden. Season with a dash of salt and black pepper.

3. Grease a cast iron skillet with 1 tablespoon of olive oil.

4. On a flat surface, dust lightly with flour. Add the pizza dough and roll until 8 inches in diameter. Transfer into the cast iron skillet.

5. Spread a thin layer of the barbecue sauce over the dough. Make sure to leave ½ an inch of the border for the crust.

6. Top off with a sprinkling of the shredded cheddar cheese, fontina cheese, cooked chicken and sliced onion.

7. Drizzle 1 tablespoon of olive oil over the top. Season with a dash of salt and black pepper.

8. Place into the oven to bake for 20 to 25 minutes or until the crust is golden.

9. Remove and drizzle ranch dressing and barbecue sauce over the top. Garnish with the chopped chives.

Mexican Pizza

Make this pizza dish whenever you are craving authentic Mexican cuisine. Made with hearty ground beef, beans, salsa and plenty of cheese, it is packed with an authentic Mexican flavor I know you will love

Makes: 8 servings

Total Prep Time: 45 minutes

Ingredients:

- ½ pound of ground beef
- 1 onion, chopped
- 1 clove of garlic, minced
- 1 Tbsp. of powdered chili
- 1 tsp. of ground chili
- ½ tsp. of smoked paprika
- Dash of black pepper
- 1, 16 ounce can of refried beans
- 4, 10 inch flour tortillas
- ½ cup of mild salsa
- 1 cup of cheddar cheese
- 1 cup of Monterey jack cheese
- 2 green onions, chopped
- 2 Roma tomatoes, chopped
- ¼ cup of jalapeno pepper, sliced thinly
- ¼ cup of sour cream, optional

Directions:

1. Heat up the oven to 350 degrees. Grease 2 pie plates with cooking spray.

2. In a skillet set over medium to high heat, add in the ground beef, chopped onion and minced garlic. Stir well to mix. Cook for 8 to 10 minutes or until browned. Drain the excess grease. Season with the powdered chili, ground cumin, smoked paprika, dash of salt and dash of black pepper.

3. Place a tortilla into the pie plates. Cover with a layer of beans. Spread half of the beef over the beans. Cover with a tortilla.

4. Place into the oven to bake for 10 minutes. Remove and set aside to cool.

5. Spread half of the mild salsa over the tortillas. Sprinkle the shredded cheddar and Monterey jack cheese over the top.

6. Add half of the tomatoes, half of the chopped green onions and half of the jalapenos over the top.

7. Place into the oven to bake for 5 to 10 minutes.

8. Remove and cool for 5 minutes before serving.

Veggie Vegetarian Pizza

This is the perfect dish for you to make whenever you are looking to impress your vegetarian friends and family.

Makes: 4 servings

Total Prep Time: 45 minutes

Ingredients:

- 1 head of cauliflower, chopped and steamed
- 1 egg, beaten
- 2 cups of mozzarella cheese, shredded and evenly divided
- ½ cup of parmesan cheese, grated and evenly divided
- ½ of a lemon, zest only
- Dash of salt and black pepper
- ¼ cup of Ragu alfredo sauce
- 1 clove of garlic, thinly sliced
- ¼ cup of red onion, thinly sliced
- ¼ cup of cherry tomatoes, cut into halves
- 1 zucchini, shaved into thin ribbons
- Basil, torn and for garnish

Directions:

1. Preheat the oven to 425 degrees.

2. In a food processor, add in the steamed cauliflower. Pulse on the highest setting until grated finely. Squeeze out as much of the liquid as possible. Transfer into a bowl.

3. In the bowl, add in the beaten egg, 1 cup of the shredded mozzarella cheese, ¼ cup of the grated Parmesan cheese and fresh lemon zest. Season with a dash of salt and black pepper. Stir well until evenly mixed.

4. Transfer the dough onto a baking sheet lined with a sheet of parchment paper. Shape into a crust that is 8 inches or less in diameter.

5. Place into the oven to bake for 20 minutes or until golden.

6. Remove and top off with the alfredo sauce, remaining mozzarella cheese, remaining parmesan cheese, sliced garlic, sliced red onion, cherry tomatoes and shaved zucchini.

7. Place back into the oven to bake for 10 minutes or until crispy.

8. Remove and serve with a garnish of torn basil.

Vegetable Pizza

This is the perfect pizza dish for you to make whenever you are trying to increase your daily intake of veggies. Every vegan and vegetarian will gush over this dish.

Makes: 12 servings

Total Prep Time: 1 hour

Ingredients:

- 2, 8 ounce packs of crescent rolls
- 2, 8 ounce packs of cream cheese, soft
- 1 cup of mayonnaise
- 1, 1 ounce pack of Ranch dressing mix
- 1 cup of broccoli, chopped
- 1 cup of tomatoes, chopped
- 1 cup of chopped green bell pepper
- 1 cup of cauliflower, chopped
- 1 cup of carrots, shredded
- 1 cup of cheddar cheese, shredded

Directions:

1. Heat up the oven to 375 degrees.

2. Roll out the crescent rolls onto a baking sheet. Pinch the edges together to form a pizza crust.

3. Place into the oven to bake for 10 to 12 minutes. Remove and set aside to cool for 15 minutes.

4. In a bowl, add in the soft cream cheese, mayo and Ranch dressing. Stir well until smooth in consistency. Spread over the crust.

5. Top off with the chopped broccoli, chopped tomato, chopped green bell pepper, chopped cauliflower, shredded carrots and shredded cheddar cheese.

6. Cover and place into the fridge to chill for 1 hour before serving.

Low Carb Breakfast Pizza

Just as the name implies, this is a delicious pizza dish that you can make early in the morning. It is the perfect dish for you to make whenever you need a boost of carbs to get you going in the morning.

Makes: 1 to 2 servings

Total Prep Time: 30 minutes

Ingredients:

- 4 eggs, beaten
- 2 ½ cup of mozzarella cheese, shredded and evenly divided
- ¼ cup of parmesan cheese, grated and extra for garnish
- Dash of salt and black pepper
- ¼ tsp. of dried oregano
- Dash of crushed red pepper flakes, optional
- 2 Tbsp. of pizza sauce
- ¼ cup of miniature pepperoni
- ½ of a green bell pepper, chopped

Directions:

1. Preheat the oven to 400 degrees. Line a baking sheet with a sheet of parchment paper.

2. In a bowl, add in the beaten eggs, 2 cups of shredded mozzarella cheese and grated parmesan cheese. Season with the crushed red pepper flakes, dried oregano, dash of salt and dash of black pepper. Sir well until mixed.

3. Place onto the baking sheet and shape into ½ inch thick round crust.

4. Spread the pizza sauce over the top.

5. Sprinkle the remaining shredded mozzarella cheese, miniature pepperoni and chopped green bell pepper over the top.

6. Place into the oven to bake for 10 minutes or until crispy.

7. Serve with a garnish of extra grated Parmesan cheese.

Thai Chicken Pizza

This is a delicious dish you can make whenever you are craving homemade Thai cuisine. It is incredibly easy to make and has a spicy punch that I know you will love.

Makes: 8 servings

Total Prep Time: 20 minutes

Ingredients:

- 1, 12 inch pizza crust, pre-baked
- 1, 7 ounce jar of peanut sauce
- ¼ cup of peanut butter
- 8 ounces of cooked chicken breasts, skinless, boneless and cut into strips
- 1 cup of Italian cheese blend, shredded
- 1 bunch of green onions, chopped
- ½ cup of bean sprouts, optional
- ½ cup of carrot, shredded and optional
- 1 Tbsp. of roasted peanuts, optional and chopped

Directions:

1. Preheat the oven to 400 degrees.

2. In a bowl, add in the peanut sauce and peanut butter. Stir well until creamy in consistency. Spread this mix over the prebaked pizza crust.

3. Add the cooked chicken strips over the sauce. Top off with the chopped green onions and shredded Italian cheese blend.

4. Place into the oven to bake for 10 to 12 minutes.

5. Remove. Top off with the bean sprouts, shredded carrots and roasted peanuts. Serve.

Pickle Pizza

This is a savory pizza dish for you to make if you love the taste of pickles. It is so delicious, I know you won't be able to help but fall in love with it.

Makes: 4 to 6 servings

Total Prep Time: 30 minutes

Ingredients:

- 1 pizza crust
- 2 Tbsp. of extra virgin olive oil
- 1 tsp. of powdered garlic
- 1 tsp. of Italian seasoning
- 1 ½ cup of mozzarella cheese, shredded
- ¼ cup of Parmesan cheese, grated
- ½ cup of pickles, thinly sliced
- 1 Tbsp. of dill, chopped
- ½ tsp. of crushed red pepper flakes
- Ranch dressing, for serving

Directions:

1. Heat the oven to 375 degrees. Place a sheet of parchment paper onto a large baking sheet.

2. In a bowl, add in the olive oil, powdered garlic and Italian seasoning. Stir well to mix.

3. Transfer the pizza crust onto a baking sheet. Brush the surface with the oil mix.

4. Top off with the shredded mozzarella cheese and grated Parmesan cheese.

5. Place into the oven to bake for 15 minutes or until melted. Remove and top off with the pickle slices. Place back into the oven to bake for an additional 5 minutes.

6. Remove and serve with a garnish of chopped dill, crushed red pepper flakes and a drizzling of the Ranch dressing.

Spinach and Alfredo Pizza

This is a special kind of pizza that you can enjoy practically every day. It is made with a topping of spinach, mushrooms and artichokes to make a meal that is hard to resist.

Makes: 16 servings

Total Prep Time: 50 minutes

Ingredients:

- 1, 10 ounce pack of spinach, frozen and thawed
- 1, 10 ounce jar of Alfredo sauce
- 1, 6 ounce can of mushrooms, thinly sliced
- 1, 10 ounce can of artichoke hearts, drained and cut into quarters
- ½ cup of grated Parmesan cheese
- 4 cups of mozzarella cheese, shredded
- 2 pizza crusts, unbaked
- 2 Tbsp. of extra virgin olive oil
- 1, 2.25 ounce can of black olives, thinly sliced and optional

Directions:

1. Heat up the oven to 350 degrees. Place the unbaked pizza crusts onto two baking sheets.

2. In a saucepan set over medium to high heat, add in the thawed spinach and alfredo sauce. Stir well to mix. Cook for 3 minutes. Remove from heat.

3. Spread 1 tablespoon of the extra virgin olive oil over the pizza crusts. Pour half of the alfredo and spinach mix over both crusts.

4. Sprinkle the artichoke hearts, half of the mozzarella cheese, sliced mushrooms, grated parmesan cheese and black olives over the sauce.

5. Place into the oven to bake for 20 minutes or until the bottom is brown.

6. Remove and serve immediately.

Four Cheese Margherita Pizza

This is a delicious twist on a classic Italian pizza I know you won't be able to resist. The feta cheese used on this pizza helps to give it a rich flavor that is nearly impossible to resist.

Makes: 8 servings

Total Prep Time: 40 minutes

Ingredients:

- ¼ cup of extra virgin olive oil
- 1 Tbsp. of garlic, minced
- ½ tsp. of sea salt
- 8 Roma tomatoes, thinly sliced
- 2, 12 inch pizza crusts, pre-baked
- 8 ounces of mozzarella cheese, shredded
- 4 ounces of Fontina cheese, shredded
- 10 basil leaves
- ½ cup of Parmesan cheese, grated
- ½ cup of feta cheese, crumbled

Directions:

1. In a bowl, add in the extra virgin olive oil, minced garlic and dash of sea salt. Add in the tomatoes and toss well to mix. Cover and set aside to rest for 15 minutes.

2. Heat up the oven to 400 degrees.

3. Brush the pizza crusts with the tomato mix.

4. Sprinkle the shredded mozzarella and fontina cheese over the top. Add a topping of the basil leaves, grated Parmesan cheese and crumbled feta cheese.

5. Place into the oven to bake for 10 minutes or until golden.

6. Remove and serve immediately.

Sausage Pizza Sliders

If you need to prepare an appetizer for your next party, then this is one dish I know you will want to make. Feel free to top off with your favorite toppings for the tastiest results.

Makes: 4 servings

Total Prep Time: 25 minutes

Ingredients:

- 9 slider buns
- 4 sweet Italian sausage links
- 12 slices of mozzarella cheese
- 1 cup of marinara
- 1 Tbsp. of butter, melted
- 2 Tbsp. of parsley, chopped and extra for garnish
- 2 Tbsp. of grated Parmesan cheese, extra for garnish

Directions:

1. Preheat the oven to 350 degrees. Grease a baking dish with cooking spray.

2. Place the bottoms of the slider buns into the baking dish.

3. In a skillet set over medium to high heat, grease with cooking spray. Add in the Italian sausage. Cook for 8 to 10 minutes or until browned. Transfer onto a flat surface and allow to rest for 5 minutes.

4. On the bottom portions of the slider buns, add a layer of the mozzarella cheese, sausage and 1 tablespoon of marinara. Cover with the top portions of the buns.

5. Cover with a sheet of aluminum foil. Place into the oven to bake for 10 minutes. Remove the foil and continue to bake for 5 minutes or until the tops are gold.

6. Remove. Garnish with the chopped parsley and grated Parmesan cheese before serving.

Classic Chicken Alfredo Pizza

One bite of this pizza dish and I know you will become hooked. Smothered in plenty of alfredo sauce, this is a pizza I know you will want to make it nearly every night.

Makes: 8 servings

Total Prep Time: 50 minutes

Ingredients for the sauce:

- 4 Tbsp. of butter
- ¼ tsp. of salt
- Dash of black pepper
- 4 Tbsp. of all-purpose flour
- 1 cup of whole milk
- ¾ cup of Romano cheese, grated

Ingredients for the garlic butter:

- 2 Tbsp. of butter
- 1 clove of garlic, minced
- Dash of dried rosemary
- Dash of salt

Ingredients for the dough:

- 1 cup of warm water
- 1, .25 ounce pack of instant yeast
- 2 Tbsp. of vegetable oil
- 1 Tbsp. of white sugar
- ½ tsp. of salt
- ¼ tsp. od dried rosemary
- ¼ tsp. of powdered garlic
- 3 cups of all-purpose flour
- 2 chicken breasts, boneless, skinless, cut into halves and roasted
- ¼ tsp. of dried rosemary
- ¼ tsp. of dried thyme
- ¼ tsp. of poultry seasoning
- ¼ tsp. of powdered garlic
- ¼ tsp. of salt

Directions:

1. Prepare the sauce. In a saucepan set over medium to high heat, add in the butter. Add in the all-purpose flour and cook for 1 minute. Add in the whole milk and grated Romano cheese. Stir well to mix. Continue to cook for 5 minutes or until thick in consistency. Season with a dash of salt and black pepper. Remove from heat and set aside.

2. Prepare the butter. In a separate saucepan set over medium to high heat, add in the butter. Add in the minced garlic, dried rosemary and dash of salt. Stir well to mix. Cook for 5 minutes or until browned. Remove from heat and set aside.

3. Prepare the dough. In a bowl, add in the water and yeast. Stir well until the dough is dissolved. Set aside to rest for 5 minutes or until foamy.

4. In a separate bowl, add in the vegetable oil, white sugar, dried rosemary and powdered garlic. Season with a dash of salt. Stir well to mix. Pour into the yeast mix. Add in the flour and stir well until a ball begins to form.

5. Transfer the dough onto a greased surface. Knead the dough for 1 to 2 minutes or until the dough is smooth. Cover and set the dough aside to rest for 30 minutes.

6. Preheat the oven to 400 degrees.

7. Season the chicken with the dried rosemary, dried thyme, poultry seasoning, powdered garlic and dash of salt. Set aside.

8. Place the pizza dough onto a pizza pan and spread until a large circle forms. Top the dough off with the garlic butter. Spread the alfredo sauce over the dough. Top off with the roasted chicken.

9. Place into the oven to bake for 20 minutes or until the curst is browned.

10. Remove and rest for 5 minutes before serving.

Pizza Nachos

If you love nachos but are wanting to impress your friends and family with your cooking skills, then this is a dish you need to make for yourself.

Makes: 6 to 8 servings

Total Prep Time: 25 minutes

Ingredients:

- 1 bag of tortilla chips
- 2 cups of pizza sauce
- 3 cups of mozzarella cheese, shredded
- 1 green bell pepper, chopped
- 1 cup of miniature pepperoni
- ½ cup of black olives, thinly sliced
- ½ cup of grated Parmesan cheese
- Parsley, chopped and for garnish

Directions:

1. Heat up the oven to 375 degrees. Line a baking sheet with a sheet of aluminum foil.

2. On the baking sheet, add half of the tortilla chips.

3. Drizzle half of the pizza sauce over the tortilla chips. Top off with half of the shredded mozzarella cheese, half of the miniature pepperoni, chopped green bell pepper, sliced black olives and grated Parmesan cheese. Repeat this layer one more time.

4. Place into the oven to bake for 15 minutes or until the cheese is fully melted.

5. Remove. Garnish the top with the parsley. Serve.

Deep Dish Alfredo Pizza

This is a delicious pizza dish I know the entire family will love. Made with a rich and creamy flavor, even the pickiest of eaters will love it.

Makes: 8 servings

Total Prep Time: 2 hours and 45 minutes

Ingredients:

- 1 cup of warm water
- ¼ cup of vegetable oil
- 1, .25 ounce pack of active yeast
- 2 cups of all-purpose flour
- ½ a pint of heavy whipping cream
- ½ cup of butter
- 2 Tbsp. of cream cheese
- ¾ cup of Parmesan cheese, grated
- 1 tsp. of powdered garlic
- 1 ½ cups of mozzarella cheese, shredded

Directions:

1. In a bowl, add in the warm water, vegetable oil and active yeast. Stir well until the yeast dissolves. Set aside to rest for 5 minutes or until foamy.

2. Add in the all-purpose flour. Stir well until a soft dough begins to form. Transfer the bowl into a greased bowl. Cover and set aside to rest for 1 hour.

3. Grease a deep dish pizza pan.

4. Transfer the dough into the pan and cover. Set aside to rest for 25 minutes or until puffed.

5. Preheat the oven to 450 degrees.

6. In a saucepan set over low to medium heat, add in the heavy whipping creamy, butter and soft cream cheese. Stir well until smooth in consistency. Add in the grated Parmesan cheese and powdered garlic. Stir well until evenly mixed. Cook for 15 minutes or until light browned. Remove and spread over the pizza crust.

7. Sprinkle the shredded mozzarella cheese over the top.

8. Place into the oven to bake for 35 minutes or until browned.

9. Remove and serve immediately.

Loaded Pizza Stromboli

This is a classic Italian dish that you can make for your next Italian night. Packed with an authentic Italian flavor, the entire family will be begging you for seconds.

Makes: 4 to 6 servings

Total Prep Time: 35 minutes

Ingredients:

- 1 pound of pizza dough
- ½ cup of Ragu marinara sauce
- 4 slices of deli ham
- 24 slices of pepperoni
- 2 ounces of cremini mushrooms, thinly sliced
- ½ of a green bell pepper, chopped
- 1 cup of mozzarella cheese, shredded
- 1 egg, beaten
- 1 Tbsp. of grated Parmesan cheese
- ½ tsp. of Italian seasoning

Directions:

1. Heat the oven to 425 degrees. Line a baking sheet with a sheet of parchment paper.

2. Stretch the pizza dough into a large rectangle. Place onto the baking sheet.

3. Spread the marinara sauce over the crust. Make sure to leave 1 inch clear around the perimeter for the crust.

4. Add a topping of the deli ham, pepperoni slices, sliced cremini mushrooms and shredded mozzarella cheese. Brush the crust with the beaten egg.

5. Roll the dough jellyroll style and pinch the edges to seal. Brush the surface with the beaten eggs. Transfer onto the baking sheet.

6. Sprinkle the grated Parmesan cheese and Italian seasoning over the top.

7. Place into the oven to bake for 25 to 30 minutes or until gold. Remove and rest for 5 minutes before serving.

Classic New York Pizza

There is just nothing like the taste of authentic New York style pizza. Topped off with plenty of mozzarella cheese and basil, this will soon become your favorite pizza.

Makes: 4 servings

Total Prep Time: 1 hour and 25 minutes

Ingredients:

- 1 tsp. of active yeast
- 2/3 cup of warm water
- 2 cups of all-purpose flour
- 1 tsp. of salt
- 1, 10 ounce can of tomato sauce
- 1 pound of mozzarella cheese, shredded
- 12 cup of Romano cheese, grated
- ¼ cup of basil, chopped
- 1 Tbsp. of dried oregano
- 1 tsp. of crushed red pepper flakes
- 2 Tbsp. of extra virgin olive oil

Directions:

1. In a bowl, add in the water and active yeast. Stir well until the yeast dissolves. Set aside to rest for 5 minutes or until foamy.

2. Add in the all-purpose flour, dash of salt and olive oil. Stir well to mix.

3. Transfer the dough onto a greased surface. Knead the dough for 5 minutes. Transfer into a greased bowl. Cover and set aside to rest for 30 minutes.

4. Heat up the oven to 475 degrees.

5. Transfer the dough onto a greased surface. Roll into a circle that is 12 inches in diameter. Transfer onto a pizza pan.

6. Spread the sauce over the pizza dough.

7. Sprinkle the dried oregano, shredded mozzarella cheese, chopped basil, grated Romano cheese and crushed red pepper flakes over the top.

8. Place into the oven to bake for 10 to 15 minutes or until the crust is browned.

9. Remove and cool for 5 minutes before serving.

Chicken Pizza Burgers

Make these delicious burgers whenever you are hosting your next family barbecue. Serve with French fries for the tastiest results.

Makes: 4 servings

Total Prep Time: 30 minutes

Ingredients:

- 1 pound of ground chicken
- 2 cloves of garlic, minced
- ¼ cup of parsley, chopped
- ¼ tsp. of crushed red pepper flakes
- Dash of salt and black pepper
- 2 Tbsp. of canola oil
- 4 slices of mozzarella cheese
- 16 slices of pepperoni
- 1 cup of Ragu marinara sauce
- 4 hamburger buns
- Basil, torn and for garnish

Directions:

1. In a bowl, add in the ground chicken, minced garlic, chopped parsley and crushed red pepper flakes. Stir well to mix. Season with a dash of salt and black pepper.

2. Shape into 4 patties.

3. In a skillet set over medium to high heat, add in the canola oil. Add in the patties and cook for 8 to 10 minutes or until gold.

4. Top the burgers with a slice of mozzarella cheese and pepperoni slices. Cover and allow to steam for 2 minutes.

5. Transfer onto the burger buns.

6. Spread a dollop of the marinara sauce over the patties.

7. Garnish with the torn basil and serve.

Beer Pizza

This is the perfect dish for you to make for those over the age of 21. It is perfect to make whenever you need to treat yourself to something special.

Makes: 16 servings

Total Prep Time: 55 minutes

Ingredients:

- 1 Tbsp. of extra virgin olive oil
- ½ pound of pepperoni sausage, chopped
- 1 pound of bacon, chopped
- 1, 4 ounce can of mushrooms, drained and thinly sliced
- 1 onion, chopped
- 1 green bell pepper, chopped
- 1, 28 ounce can of tomato sauce
- 1 cup of dark beer
- 1 clove of garlic, minced
- 1 tsp. of dried oregano
- ½ tsp. of dried thyme
- ½ tsp. of salt
- 2 pizza crusts, unbaked
- 1, 8 ounce pack of mozzarella cheese, shredded

Directions:

1. Heat up the oven to 450 degrees.

2. In a skillet set over medium to high heat, add in the pepperoni sausage and chopped bacon. Stir well to mix. Cook for 5 minutes or until browned.

3. Add in the can of sliced mushrooms, chopped onion and chopped green bell pepper. Stir well to mix. Cook for 5 minutes or until soft.

4. In a separate saucepan set over medium heat, add in the veggie mix, tomato sauce and dark beer. Stir gently to mix. Add in the minced garlic, dried oregano, dried thyme and a dash of salt. Stir well to mix. Cook for 15 minutes or until thick in consistency.

5. Spread the mix over the pizza crusts. Sprinkle the shredded mozzarella cheese over the top.

6. Place the crusts onto a pizza pan. Place into the oven to bake for 20 to 25 minutes or until golden.

7. Remove and serve immediately.

Barbecue Chicken Pizza Sliders

This is another great tasting pizza dish you can serve during your next lunch or dinner event. It is so delicious, your guests will be begging you for the recipe.

Makes: 4 to 6 servings

Total Prep Time: 35 minutes

Ingredients:

- 12 Hawaiian rolls
- 3 cups of rotisserie chicken, shredded
- ½ cup of barbecue sauce
- ¼ cup of red onion, chopped
- ¼ cup of cilantro, chopped
- 3 slices of cheddar cheese
- ¼ cup of butter, melted
- 1 clove of garlic, minced
- 1 tsp. of powdered onion

Directions:

1. Preheat the oven to 350 degrees.

2. Separate the Hawaiian rolls into halves. Place the bottom halves into a baking dish.

3. In a bowl, add in the shredded rotisserie chicken and barbecue sauce. Stir well to evenly coat. Spoon onto the bottom half of the Hawaiian rolls.

4. Sprinkle the red onion and chopped cilantro over the top.

5. Slices the slices of cheddar cheese into 4 pieces and place over the top of each slider.

6. Cover with the tops of the Hawaiian rolls.

7. In a bowl, add in the melted butter and powdered garlic. Stir well to mix. Brush the tops of the sliders with this mix.

8. Place into the oven to bake for 15 minutes while covered with a sheet of aluminum foil.

9. Remove and serve immediately.

Ham, Egg and Cheese Pizza

Make this delicious pizza whenever you are craving breakfast for dinner. It is an incredibly simple pizza dish you can make, even those with little cooking skill can make it with ease.

Makes: 4 servings

Total Prep Time: 25 minutes

Ingredients:

- 1 pound of pizza dough, store-bought
- 1 Tbsp. of extra virgin olive oil, extra for greasing
- 2 cups of mozzarella cheese, shredded
- 1 cup of ham, chopped
- 5 eggs
- Dash of black pepper
- Parsley, chopped and for garnish

Directions:

1. Heat up the oven to 425 degrees. Grease a pizza pan with olive oil.

2. Roll the pizza dough onto the pizza pan. Spread the remaining olive oil over the top of the crusts.

3. Sprinkle the shredded mozzarella cheese and chopped ham over the top.

4. Crack the eggs directly over the top. Season with a dash of black pepper.

5. Place into the oven to bake for 15 minutes or until the eggs are set.

6. Remove and serve with a garnish of chopped parsley.

Breakfast Cornbread Pizza

This is another delicious breakfast pizza dish you can make whenever you need something tasty to get you going early in the morning.

Makes: 6 servings

Total Prep Time: 45 minutes

Ingredients:

- 1 box of Jiffy corn muffin mix
- 1 egg
- ½ cup of sour cream
- 1 cup of cheddar cheese, shredded
- 6 slices of bacon, cut into small pieces
- 6 eggs
- Dash of salt and black pepper
- 2 green onions, thinly sliced

Directions:

1. Preheat the oven to 400 degrees. Grease a cast iron skillet with cooking spray.

2. In a bowl, add in the corn muffin mix, 1 egg and sour cream. Stir well until smooth in consistency. Transfer into the cast iron skillet.

3. Place into the oven to bake for 15 to 20 minutes or until gold.

4. In a separate skillet set over medium to high heat, add in the bacon pieces. Cook for 5 minutes or until crispy. Remove from heat and transfer onto a plate lined with paper towels to drain.

5. Over the cornbread, crack the remaining 6 eggs directly over the top. Sprinkle the chopped bacon over the top. Season with a dash of salt and black pepper.

6. Place into the oven to bake for 15 minutes or until the eggs are set.

7. Remove and serve with a garnish of sliced green onions.

Miniature Deep Dish Pizzas

These pizzas are perfect to make during your next lunch or dinner event. Topped off with chopped basil and packed full of cheese, your guests won't be able to resist it.

Makes: 12 servings

Total Prep Time: 25 minutes

Ingredients:

- 4, 8 inch flour tortillas
- 1 cup of pizza sauce
- ¾ cup of mozzarella cheese, shredded
- ¼ cup of Parmesan cheese, grated
- 48 slices of miniature pepperoni
- 2 Tbsp. of basil, chopped

Directions:

1. Heat up the oven to 425 degrees. Grease a miniature muffin pan with cooking spray.

2. Place a tortilla onto a flat surface. Cut out 3 rounds from the tortilla and place into the bottom of the muffin cups. Repeat with the remaining tortillas.

3. Add 1 tablespoon of the pizza sauce into the muffin cups. Sprinkle the shredded mozzarella cheese and grated Parmesan cheese into the cups. Top off with 3 to 5 slices of miniature pepperoni.

4. Place into the oven to bake for 10 to 15 minutes.

5. Remove and serve immediately with a garnish of chopped basil.

Pizza Puffs

These are the perfect treats to make whenever you need to prepare an appetizer for your next family gathering. One bite and your friends and family will be begging for the recipe.

Makes: 12 servings

Total Prep Time: 35 minutes

Ingredients:

- 3 cups of Bisquick
- 2 eggs
- 1 cup of whole milk
- 3 Tbsp. of extra virgin olive oil
- 2 tsp. of Italian seasoning
- ¾ tsp. of salt
- ½ tsp. of powdered garlic
- ¾ cup of miniature pepperoni, extra for garnish
- ½ cup of Parmesan cheese, grated and extra for garnish
- 8 ounces of mozzarella string cheese, sliced into thirds
- Marinara sauce, for dipping

Directions:

1. Heat up the oven to 400 degrees. Grease a muffin pan with cooking spray.

2. In a bowl, add in the Bisquick, eggs, whole milk, extra virgin olive oil, powdered garlic and Italian seasoning. Season with a dash of salt. Stir well to mix.

3. Add in the miniature pepperoni and grated Parmesan cheese. Fold gently to incorporate.

4. Pour into the muffin cups.

5. Press a piece of the mozzarella string cheese into the center of the batter in the muffin cups. Top off with the miniature pepperoni.

6. Place into the oven to bake for 20 minutes or until gold.

7. Remove and garnish with the grated Parmesan cheese. Serve with the marinara sauce for dipping.

Mac and Cheese Pizza

This is one pizza dish you can make for those picky children in your home. One bite and they will be begging you for seconds.

Makes: 4 servings

Total Prep Time: 40 minutes

Ingredients:

- 1 box of macaroni and cheese + ingredients listed on the box
- 1 cup of cheddar cheese, shredded and evenly divided
- 1 cup of mozzarella cheese, shredded and evenly divided
- 1 pound of pizza dough
- Extra virgin olive oil, for brushing
- ¼ tsp. of powdered garlic
- ¼ tsp. of Italian seasoning
- Dash of salt and black pepper
- Parsley, chopped and for serving

Directions:

1. Heat up the oven to 450 degrees. Place a sheet of parchment paper onto a baking sheet.

2. Prepare the box of macaroni and cheese according to the directions on the package. Once prepared, add ½ cup of the shredded cheddar cheese and ½ cup of shredded mozzarella cheese. Stir well until the cheese melts.

3. Roll the pizza dough until 12 inches in diameter. Place onto the baking sheet.

4. Brush the top of the pizza dough with the olive oil. Sprinkle the powdered garlic over the top.

5. Place into the oven to bake for 10 minutes or until golden.

6. Spread the prepared mac and cheese over the top of the crust. Make sure to leave ½ inch border for the crust.

7. Sprinkle the remaining shredded cheddar and mozzarella cheese.

8. Place back into the oven to bake for 10 minutes or until the cheese melts.

9. Remove and serve with a garnish of chopped parsley.

Conclusion

Well, there you have it!

Hopefully by the end of this book you have found plenty of pizza recipes that you can make within the comfort of your own home. By the end of this book, not only do I hope you have gained the confidence to make your very own pizza dishes from scratch but have found over 25 delicious pizza recipes that I know you will love.

So, what is next for you?

The next step for you to take is to begin making all of the pizza recipes you have discovered inside of this book. Once you have done that, it will be time for you to try your hand at making your very own pizza dishes from scratch.

Good luck!

Author's Afterthoughts

Thanks Ever So Much to Each of My Cherished Readers for Investing the Time to Read This Book!

I know you could have picked from many other books but you chose this one. So, big thanks for buying this book and reading all the way to the end.

If you enjoyed this book or received value from it, I'd like to ask you for a favor. Please take a few minutes to post an honest and heartfelt review on **Amazon.** Your support does make a difference and helps to benefit other people.

Thank you!

Carla Hale

About the Author

Carla Hale

I think of myself as a foodie. I like to eat, yes. I like to cook even more. I like to prepare meals for my family and friends, I feel like that's what I was born to do...

My name is Carla Hale and as may have suspected already, I am originally from Scotland. I am first and foremost a mother, a wife, but simultaneously over the years I became a proclaimed cook. I have shared my recipes with many and will continue to do so, as long as I can. I like different. I dress different, I love different, I speak different and I cook different. I like to think that I am different because I am more animated about what I do than most; I feel more and care more.

It served me right when cooking to sprinkle some tenderness, love, passion, in every dish I prepare. It does not matter if I am preparing a meal for strangers passing by my cooking booth at the flea market or if I am making my mother's favorite recipe. Each and every meal I prepare from scratch will contain a little bite of my life story and little part of my heart in it. People feel it, taste it and ask for more! Thank you for taking the time to get to know me and hopefully through my recipes you can learn a lot more about my influences and preferences. Who knows you might just find your own favorite within my repertoire! Enjoy!

Made in United States
Orlando, FL
01 December 2022